What Happens Next?
DEALING WITH LIFE CHANGES

What Happens When I Have a Serious Illness?

Danielle Haynes

PowerKiDS press

Published in 2025 by The Rosen Publishing Group, Inc.
2544 Clinton Street, Buffalo, NY 14224

Copyright © 2025 by The Rosen Publishing Group, Inc.

First Edition

All rights reserved. No part of this book may be reproduced in any form without permission in writing from the publisher, except by a reviewer.

Editor: Theresa Emminizer
Book Design: Leslie Taylor

Photo Credits: Cover Ground Picture/Shutterstock.com; p. 5 Andrey_Popov/Shutterstock.com; p. 7 Andrey_Popov/Shutterstock.com; p. 9 Pressmaster/Shutterstock.com; p. 11 New Africa/Shutterstock.com; p. 13 JPC-PROD/Shutterstock.com; p. 15 Monkey Business Images/Shutterstock.com; p. 17 Hananeko_Studio/Shutterstock.com; p. 19 Africa Studio/Shutterstock.com; p. 21 Ladanifer/Shutterstock.com.

Cataloging-in-Publication Data

Names: Haynes, Danielle.
Title: What happens when I have a serious illness? / Danielle Haynes.
Description: Buffalo, NY : PowerKids Press, 2025. | Series: What happens next? dealing with life changes| Includes glossary and index.
Identifiers: ISBN 9781725327139 (pbk.) | ISBN 9781725327153 (library bound) | ISBN 9781725327160 (ebook)
Subjects: LCSH: Chronic diseases–Juvenile literature. | Chronically ill–Juvenile literature.
Classification: LCC RC108.H39 2025 | DDC 616'..044-dc23

Manufactured in the United States of America

Some of the images in this book illustrate individuals who are models. The depictions do not imply actual situations or events.

CPSIA Compliance Information: Batch #CSPK25. For Further Information contact Rosen Publishing at 1-800-237-9932.

Find us on

CONTENTS

What Now? 4
What's Ailing You? 6
Diagnosis 8
Treatment 10
How Are You Feeling? 14
Serious Illness and School 16
A New Normal 20
Glossary 22
For More Information 23
Index 24

What Now?

Something doesn't feel right. Your stomach hurts. Maybe your head hurts. Maybe sometimes you just feel so tired you can't get out of bed. And when your grown-ups take you to the doctor, they **diagnose** you with a serious illness.

It sounds really scary. Your mind may be filled with lots of questions and worries. What's going to happen next? Can you still go to school?

Serious, or really bad, illnesses can greatly change your **future**. But the more you learn about your illness, the more you can deal with it!

When you go to the doctor, they'll look inside your ears, eyes, nose, and mouth with special tools. They may do lots of other tests.

5

What's Ailing You?

There are many different illnesses that can ail you, or cause you to be sick. Some make you feel bad for just a few days and then can go away. Some of these are called acute conditions. Others last a long time, maybe the rest of your life. They're called chronic diseases.

Some examples of serious or chronic illnesses are:
- cancer—the uncontrolled growth of cells in the body
- asthma—a condition that makes it hard to breathe
- diabetes—a disease in which the body can't control the glucose, or sugar, in the blood

Testing your blood sugar hurts just a little bit. Over time, many people say they get used to it.

Your Point of View

People with diabetes may test the amount of glucose in their blood by poking a small hole in their finger. A machine takes a little bit of the blood and tells the user their blood sugar level.

Diagnosis

Sometimes getting a diagnosis can be one of the scariest parts of having a serious illness. You have a doctor using all kinds of tools to look at your mouth, eyes, and other body parts. They're taking your blood, and that doesn't feel good. Maybe you need to have a picture taken inside your body. This may be a radiograph (X-ray) or magnetic resonance imaging (MRI).

Your doctor must look over all these tests to figure out what's wrong. For you and your family, waiting and being unsure of the results can be **stressful**. But it's better to know!

MRIs don't hurt, but you must lie still for 30 to 60 minutes while the machine does its work.

Your Point of View

X-rays and MRIs are both used to take a closer look inside your body. X-rays are best for taking pictures of your bones. MRIs are better for looking at soft body parts, such as your brain or heart.

Treatment

Once your doctors know what illness you have, it's time for treatment! There are lots of of treatments for different illnesses. Remember that not all (or even most) illnesses are serious, but we can still treat even these today.

Cancer, for instance, is a serious illness that may require **surgery**. Some cancers cause people to grow tumors, or masses, in their body. A tumor in your brain, for example, needs to come out. A tumor in the bone of your leg might mean you need to have your leg amputated, or removed. Many cancer surgeries are followed by **chemotherapy** for several months. This can make you feel very sick.

Chemotherapy is a very strong kind of medicine. It can cause your hair to fall out, but don't worry—it can grow back!

Your Point of View

Even though surgery and chemotherapy can make you feel worse, doctors will give you medicine to make you feel better. Make sure to always tell them how you're feeling so they can help you!

Treatments for other kinds of illnesses may be a little easier to deal with. But you may have to take these treatments for the rest of your life.

With diabetes, for example, you might have to take daily medicine to keep your blood sugar steady. You'll also have to carefully keep an eye on what you eat, because certain foods can cause glucose to go higher.

Asthma can also require daily medication. Asthmatic people also usually carry an inhaler with them all the time. This device lets you inhale, or breathe in, a puff of medicine if you're having a sudden asthma attack.

Inhalers send medicine to your lungs, easing the **inflammation** that makes it hard for asthmatic people to breathe.

13

How Are You Feeling?

Having a serious illness can hurt more than just your body. It can be hard to deal with **emotionally** too.

You might feel scared about your future. You might feel worried about any surgery you're going to have. You might be angry because you can't go to school or play outside with friends. Having someone to talk about your feelings with can help. Tell your grown-ups how you're feeling and ask them questions if you're confused about what's going on. Lean on your friends.

Moms, dads, and other family members can help comfort you when you're feeling down.

Your Point of View

Sometimes, you might need more help than your grown-ups can give. Some **therapists** are trained to help young people dealing with serious illnesses. You might find it easier to talk to them.

Serious Illness and School

Some serious illnesses will require you to miss school. If you must spend time in the hospital, you can't go to class. Your teachers might be able to send homework for you to do when you feel up to it. Some hospitals have school programs to help you keep up with school work.

You might have an illness that causes your **immune system** to be weak. If it's too dangerous for you to be around others, you might have to leave school. Homeschooling could be a good option.

Online learning is another option for kids with serious illnesses who must stay home.

17

When you do go back to school, you might need a little extra help. Some students returning from a long illness might need to redo a school year or get one-on-one help called tutoring.

Others might need an individualized education program (IEP). This is a plan with the school to make sure you get the help you need to learn. If your illness left you with hearing loss, for example, a teacher could make sure you sit at the front of class. People with other **physical** disabilities can have extra time to get to class.

Your Point of View

Missing school means missing your friends too! Try to keep in touch by phone or internet. If you're well enough, ask a grown-up if your friends can visit.

Some students attend extra classes at school to help with things such as speech after a serious illness.

A New Normal

Getting diagnosed with a serious illness can be really scary. The good news, though, is that most illnesses can be treated.

Some serious illnesses mean you now have a new way to live. You might always carry an inhaler or have to learn a new way to eat. You might have a disability that means getting a prosthesis, or fake limb. Even if you're cured of your disease, it can change you. This is normal, and it's important to talk to people about it.

Your Point of View

It's a fact of life that some serious illnesses can lead to death. There's nothing anyone can say to make that OK, especially for a young person. But leaning on your family, friends, and even a therapist can help you deal with your feelings.

Even with a prosthesis, you can still enjoy all your favorite sports and hobbies.

Glossary

chemotherapy: The use of certain chemicals to treat cancer.

diagnose: To identify a disease by its signs and symptoms.

emotional: Dealing with strong feelings.

future: Something that has yet to be.

immune system: The part of the body that protects from diseases.

inflammation: A condition in which part of your body becomes red and swollen.

physical: Relating to the body.

stressful: Causing strong feelings of worry.

surgery: A procedure carried out by a doctor that requires cutting the body.

therapist: A person trained to help people with emotional or mental problems.

For More Information

Books

Finne, Stephanie. *Facing Serious Illness*. Minneapolis, MN: Blue Owl Books, 2021.

Storm, Kelsie, and Sarah Porter. *A Kids Book About Cancer*. A Kids Book About Inc., 2021.

Websites

CHOC
health.choc.org/guide/chronic-illness/#kids
Read these helpful tips about living with a chronic illness.

Kids Health
kidshealth.org/en/kids/cancer.html
Learn more about cancer and how to cope with it.

Publisher's note to educators and parents: Our editors have carefully reviewed these websites to ensure that they are suitable for students. Many websites change frequently, however, and we cannot guarantee that a site's future contents will continue to meet our high standards of quality and educational value. Be advised that students should be closely supervised whenever they access the internet.

Index

A
asthma, 6, 12

C
cancer, 6, 10
chronic, 6

D
diabetes, 6, 7, 12
disabilities, 18

G
glucose, 6

I
inhaler, 12, 20

M
magnetic resonance imaging (MRI), 8, 9

P
prosthesis, 20, 21

T
tumor, 10

X
X-ray, 8, 9